It All Started with a Purple Guitar

To my secret garden

Author's note

Hello. *waves awkwardly*
I suppose if I'd kept any diaries between the ages of 12-22, these would be some of the pages. Hope at least one of them helps.
Also, grab a pair of headphones.

TWs: This book contains material relating to

anxiety, depression, addiction, verbal abuse, physical abuse, memory loss, childhood trauma, and possibly more

~ TABLE OF CONTENTS ~

Beginning
~ I DON'T KNOW YOUR NAME
~ A GENTLE THING
~ PRETTY ~~PATHETIC~~ DOLLHOUSE
~ DOLL ON DISPLAY
~ PAIN
~ TAP SHOES
~ SUNDAYS

Middle
~ TERROR IS CONSISTENT
~ STILL
~ PHANTOM WOUNDS
~ THORN
~ DREAMING
~ WARM WATER
~ ADDICT
~ PUZZLES
~ THE MOST COVETED SECRET
~ STARE
~ SORE THUMB
~ EMPTY CUP FEELING
~ TRAVELER
~ SEASHELLS
~ HOME IS SUBJECTIVE
~ CHAINED
~ THE GRAVEYARD
~ THE SWITCH
~ VANITY

~ TRUE LOVE
~ A WEARY HAND WANTS TO REST HERE
~ SHADOWS
~ *UNTITLED*

Now
~ THE RAINDROP ON THE WINDOW
~ MOROSE
~ ZIPPED LIPS
~ AN APOLOGY TO WHOM IT MAY CONCERN
~ A LETTER TO THE DOLL
~ TWENTY-TWO
~ MUSIC
~ MUSIC II
~ WINGS
~ THE SONGBIRD
~ PURPLE ACOUSTIC

<33
~ NEVER BEEN KISSED
~ BLINK
~ CRUSH
~ IF ONLY YOU KNEW
~ _____ AT ITS FINEST
~ MISSED OPPORTUNITIES
~ THE ANSWER TO YOUR QUESTION
~ FOR YOU
~ UNIQUE

Others
~ AUTUMN OUTFIT
~ VISIT
~ IT MOVES AGAINST MY WILL
~ RIBS
~ SANDS
~ SHE ROTS

Beginning

~ Beginning playlist ~

Dollhouse ~ Melanie Martinez
Chandelier ~ Sia
Gasoline ~ Halsey
Cool Kids ~ Echosmith
Papaoutai ~ Stromae
Secrets ~ OneRepublic
The One That Got Away ~ The Civil Wars
Counting Stars ~ OneRepublic
Radioactive ~ Imagine Dragons
Sweet Nothing (feat. Florence Welch) ~ Calvin Harris
Elastic Heart ~ Sia
Viva La Vida ~ Coldplay
Freedom ~ Pharrell Williams
Team ~ Lorde
Can't Hold Us (feat. Ray Dalton) ~ Macklemore & Ryan Lewis

I DON'T KNOW YOUR NAME

She didn't know the name of the dark figure that fought to claim the air from her lungs.
The large hands seeking to strangle life from the body of a naive child, a novice when it came to battles of this nature.
She had no weapons. She had no strategies.
She had her small hands and her small feet.
And in her young mind, she also had enough sense to know that her hands were no match for the shadow, no matter how hard they hit.
Her tiny feet kicked out relentlessly, even as she was suspended further in the air by the shadow's merciless grip on her throat. Her vision was fading. More air had escaped her than was left in her.
She was tired. Every day, hands flailing at her sides, hitting at the shadow's arms. Feet kicking and kicking that refused to cease kicking.
The shadow never finished her off, which was intentional. He just liked to stalk—slithering like a serpent in the dimness of every corner of every room—until he was ready to inflict torture once again.
It had become a routine. A dance of sorts.
She was too young to keep struggling through venomous conflict meant for seasoned soldiers.
She knew nothing of tactics. What defenses did she have?
Her heart held no desire to become battle-scarred. She just wanted to breathe.

The shadow knew all of these things. Above all, how tired she was. Which is why every time her eyes would start to fall shut and her hands would begin to lose their momentum and her fists would loosen... he would drop her.

Back on the ground she was, air forcing its way back into her lungs in large, gaping breaths. She reached a hand to her throat to rub it as the shadow turned its back on her and walked out of the room. The slow, deliberate steps of Chaos embodied.

Same time tomorrow.

Eventually, those hands painted her innocence black.

A GENTLE THING

The torture it was.
To inhabit a body that never slept. My feet had grown blistered and bloodied from chasing Sleep.
It always took the time to turn its head and laugh at the struggling girl who was never quite fast enough.
The agony it was.
To have a mind that never rested.
Nightmares welcomed me, and dreams hid from me in far places.
Twenty-four hours in a day, every hour blurred, one carrying no distinction from the previous; the sharpness of my mind had dwindled to that of a dull blade.
Day and Night were one and the same because both were just as dark.
At times, my sobs were soundless. But when they carried sound, no one would hear me anyway.
All thoughts were loud. All *silence* was loud.
Life was screaming at me, and I just wanted to tell it that I didn't understand.
I was too young to understand.
And so I wept.
With the distant hope in my heart that, one day, Life would show that little girl a kindness.
And become a very gentle thing.

PRETTY ~~PATHETIC~~ DOLLHOUSE

The pretty little girl does her mechanical wave for the congregation of petty onlookers. It's a move no one her age should have down to a fine art.
She had learned early on how to masterfully navigate this rather... *inhuman* game of politics.
And she liked to play with dolls, so becoming one hadn't been too difficult.
In the moments where the room began to feel a little more hostile than usual, the atmosphere a bit heavier, and the air in her lungs a little less dependable, she would just pretend she was at home—that she was a doll in her beautiful pink dollhouse, all nicely dressed and cared for by its owner. Because at the end of the day, she was the only one who had taken care of her.
And that special trick would work every time. With ease, the forced smile would continue to be plastered onto her face as if it had never left; her posture would remain straight; not one fragment of lint on a stitch of her clothing; not one hair on her head found out of place.
Stand up straight. *But my shoulders are heavy and I don't know why.*
Smile. *Even though I don't want to.*
Shake their hands. *I know they don't like me, but it's important to play along.*
Walk with your head held high. *"Lowest of the low" is the highest compliment I could be paid right now.*
Most importantly, do not cry. *Save the tears until we're home. I've done this a thousand times.*
It's almost over.

She looked out into the crowd again and felt a tinge of jealousy. Why do *they* get to do it?
Smudge their makeup, wrinkle their neatly pressed clothes, make a mess of their perfect haircuts.
Have the privilege of getting dirty.

What a luxury it is to be imperfect. To be human.
A luxury the little girl wanted to buy but knew she couldn't afford.
To pay that price would be to ruin everything.
Or at least, that's what her fragmented mind led her to believe.

DOLL ON DISPLAY

Being a doll had two sides.
Heavy admiration from a distance or biting envy up close, with rare middle ground.
Of course, the envious dolls took the liberty of concealing their true emotions with a strained smile or a disingenuous compliment. Dolls never change face. In spite of their emotions, their countenances never falter, never shift.
Another lesson she'd learned.
She couldn't lie; she liked to be admired. She sometimes liked the pedestal she was made to stand on. But she'd also be lying if she said it didn't get lonely up there.
Sometimes, "lonely" was all-encompassing black, a dark void, a hole she didn't have the will to keep trying to crawl out of. It edged into her bed at night and wrapped around her with arms of gloom. She never dreamed.
Other times, it was in the tedium and fraudulence of day-to-day interactions with other dolls. She was a toy that was sick of playing games. Many times, during ordinary conversations, she desperately itched to reach a thumb across one of their eyelids, curious to see if the eyeshadow would smudge. Or take a glass of water and toss it in one of their faces to see if the mascara would run.
Who was she kidding? She doubted their clothes would even get wet. They'd been at this for too long.

Bedtime. Her mirror getting the same silent pleas:

Someone remove the makeup, please.
Take me out of these inanely frilly dresses.
These stupid pins keep sticking my head.
Polished shoes, I can see *the plastic staring back at me. Why would I* choose *to wear them?*
My hands fidget with or without the white gloves on.

A knock sounded at her door. She knew it was her mother coming to say good night, and they exchanged their normal nightly biddings.
She never said that the nights hadn't been good in a while.
Coal-black nightmares sat on the edge of her bed, waiting to overtake her sleep.
The doll was no longer scared of them.

PAIN

In the sea of cutting amnesia, it was still crafty enough to leave its trace.
I cannot paint an accurate picture of what my life looked like when pain was the cornerstone on which the building of my thoughts stood. I can, however, perfectly paint the feeling.
Nothing and everything. I could hold on to nothing, but I felt everything as it slipped through my fingers. Everything good, anyway. Most things that brought pleasure or happiness were lost in that gray haze that clouded those years. Few escaped and were able to outrun the fog.
I'm grateful they were fast enough, so I could have something to hold on to.

TAP SHOES

The red curtains close.
In the moment, I feel nothing.
In that moment, I hadn't planned on letting it go.
I wasn't aware of the fact that it was the last day I'd tie up my tap shoes.
If I knew how much I'd miss them, I probably wouldn't have been so eager to take them off.
Often, I reminisce about the easy union between my two feet, the metal beneath my soles, and the floor. How all three never had any qualms between them. They had a special bond I couldn't grasp or appreciate in the midst of the storms.
If I was ever sure at any time in my life, it was back then, when I was in my tap shoes.
They're still underneath my bed, and every once in a while I ache to put them on just to feel the bond again—the old magic of ease.
I can never bring myself to do it, though. At some point in your life, you learn the art of realizing when certain things are of the past.
When the old magic should remain untouched and untainted by your nostalgic present whims.
Past loves were never meant to carry.
So, still, the laces remain loosened.

SUNDAYS

The fig tree.
The easy ripples of the pool.
The garden we never got quite right.
The easy Sundays that were Heaven in our small corner of Earth.
Adolescent gameplay.

I don't know where the old dolls are.
(That irony is not lost on me.)
I haven't seen them in eight years, since I placed them all in my wooden toy chest and said goodbye.
Before I closed the chest for the very last time, I noticed a few things. Our times of play had worn on them. They had a few nicks in their arms and legs. Their hair was dull and slightly ratty. Their clothes had torn and now their makeup was smudged.
Apparent flaws, some due to careless mishandling and others the normal flaws that come with time, the passing of it. A little bit like their owner.
All of them looked so small inside the chest. I thought about how strange that was. How these seemingly insignificant pieces of plastic that I'd held in my hands more times than I could count were so much bigger than they looked, and they'd never know it.
So full of stories. The machinations of our childlike imaginations practically bounced off of them even now, and I could still see all the dreams we said out loud and the ones we never did; they burned bright in our eyes, and the flames met whenever we looked at each other, so we didn't have to. No one could tell us we didn't exceed the "Welcome to _____" and soar past the state lines.

The dolls: seemingly insignificant, small, flawed.
Before I closed the chest for the very last time, I noticed one thing.

They stopped being my toys a long time ago. Somewhere along the way, between them getting their scars and me getting mine, I no longer saw dolls. I saw mirror images.
The scars on them had made me feel better about the scars in me.
I no longer saw dolls. I saw timeworn acquaintances that understood where I was coming from because we looked just alike.
Understanding. That's why goodbyes are always hard.

The fig tree.
The easy ripples of the pool.
The garden we never got quite right.
The easy Sundays that were Heaven in our small corner of Earth.
Adolescent gameplay that was never just gameplay.

Middle

~ Middle playlist ~

Paradise ~ Coldplay
E.T. ~ Katy Perry, Kanye West
Glory and Gore ~ Lorde
Bad Dream ~ Ruelle
idontwannabeyouanymore ~ Billie Eilish
fake smile ~ Ariana Grande
Here ~ Alessia Cara
Rather Be (feat. Jess Glynne) ~ Clean Bandit
Maps ~ Maroon 5
Fourth of July ~ Fall Out Boy
Water Fountain ~ Alec Benjamin
Let Me Down Slowly ~ Alec Benjamin
bellyache ~ Billie Eilish
Out of My League (The Voice performance) ~ Troy Ritchie
Doubt ~ Twenty One Pilots
I Fall Apart ~ Post Malone
watch ~Billie Eilish
Cross My Mind ~ ARIZONA
Renegades ~ X Ambassadors
Ride ~ Twenty One Pilots
Wide Awake ~ Katy Perry
Changes ~ Dej Loaf

TERROR IS CONSISTENT

What was scarier: Being asleep or being awake?
The girl didn't know.
She'd spent her days in the misery of a high-alert agony. Every minute felt like walking a tightrope between peace and destruction.
During the days, she'd oddly never thought about how strange it was that her eyes were always darting, or that she flinched at the tiniest speck of whatever was floating in the air. She didn't find it strange that trivial noises induced life-and-death reactions.
She also didn't find it odd that her head, dark as it was, had become her favorite hiding place.
The nightmares, she didn't find strange either. After a while, in a warped way, they felt normal. It would've been stranger if horror hadn't woken her up in the dead of night in cold sweats and kept her eyes open until sunrise.
She didn't see anything wrong with any of it.
She just wanted to control Pain.
Pain only scared her when it became unpredictable. That's when the terror would set in.
So, she'd deal with the unnecessary daytime alertness that had become habitual and the nighttime monsters that had become common. She could handle them.
As long as they no longer caught her off guard.

STILL

Sorrow was the thing that made her stand still. It stunted every movement she dared her bones to make. It brought her to her knees and made her curl up within herself.

There she lay on the ground. Begging her limbs to move… urging her legs to get up. Looking deep within herself to find the light that once made them do so with the unworried spirit of a child walking through life.

Perhaps she'd gone blind. But she was past the point of caring. It's hard to when you're heavy.

PHANTOM WOUNDS

Still hurt.
When the stones are thrown, my screams are ignored and deaf ears
are turned to the raw cries that escape my throat.
As if I've done something to deserve the eagerness behind the hands.

THORN

I pray to receive a thorn in my flesh. A thorn is isolated.
These wounds cover me.

DREAMING

"Dreaming."
Definition: The rabbit hole, where the vibrant makings of my imagination descend to be laid waste.

WARM WATER

I don't feel the warmth of the water that surrounds me.
I feel lost.
What brand of broken do you have to be to end up like this?
Hot, cold. The same.
Happy, sad. No difference.
I can't say that I'm a shell of my former self because I've never been more than this.

I was born bent. Pressure may make diamonds, but it also breaks levees.
It was only a matter of time.

ADDICT

A definition of 'addict': a devoted fan.
(Willing ears listening to jagged lies coated with dripping honey.)

I tasted something poisonous.
In my defense, I wasn't aware. Not really.
Not until after.
To my demise, it tasted good. Everything tastes better when it's too late.
The effects hit as soon as it went down.
That's when I first felt the ravens.
The first hint of them, the breeze of their wings brushing against me.
I felt one drag along my shoulder. I didn't turn around, but the hint of black I'd caught from a sideways glance was enough.
I was dying already.

The first time wasn't *that* bad. (*A hideous lie.*)
The effects could've been worse. (*Ugly. I feel so ugly. A disgusting waste.*)

I went back to the poison.
I am a bit disappointed, though. *(It bothers me that I'm breathing.)*
It tastes slightly different. Not as good as it was. (*I should've died the first time.*

I went back to the poison.

PUZZLES

Can I confess something in the form of a question?
Have you ever felt like the puzzle piece that didn't fit?
You know how puzzles go: all of the different pieces scattered across the same table. They're alike, but each of them is wholly distinct. Their distinctions don't matter because you know eventually they're all going to fit together and create a beautiful picture, like the box shows. You don't think of putting one piece in place of another—the completed puzzle won't look right.
I don't know.
Sometimes, I feel like I've been carved differently, shaped with too much distinction to fit into any place without feeling how much it wasn't made for me.

THE MOST COVETED SECRET

(There's a reason for my tears, and it's this.)
I wonder every day what it feels like.
When the wonder is no longer necessary.
To no longer have to imagine, but to have.

I want to be let in on the secret of Happiness.

STARE

I look for eyes that don't set me on edge.
I'm met with many pairs daily; they feel less like eyes and more like desperate weapons—freshly-sharpened and primed to attack with murderous aim.
Daggers are zeroed in at my throat, but the vain effort to protect the poor façades of warm-heartedness keep them from attempting to draw my blood.

Eyes that are blades, followed by a kind word that's a well wish dripping with veiled venom.
I wish I could meet more eyes that are truly kind to me.

SORE THUMB

If you ask the average person why a sore thumb sticks out, they'd probably say it's because
it's red.
It's swollen.
The thumb is the largest finger on the hand; it's impossible to avoid.
All true answers. But in my opinion, none of them are correct. Not completely, at least. I don't think a sore thumb sticks out for any of those reasons alone. I think it's sticking out because it's hurting.
This is the part where you say "duh." But let me explain.
When you first hear the expression, the focus is automatically on the results of the thumb's soreness and the appearance it takes on after it's been injured. No one bothers to wonder how it got hurt. It's judged for the appearance it takes on after it's been wounded, so much that the judgment has become a commonplace saying.
Or maybe these are simply the overthought ramblings of a person who's been in the thumb's shoes before.

EMPTY CUP FEELING

Exasperation that results from the culmination of a lot of little things about a lot of little things that feel like big things because you're devoid of what you need to keep pouring.

TRAVELER

She longed to walk the miles her heart had traveled already.

SEASHELLS

She kept them as reminders of what freedom looked like. Tangible reminders of the air she ached to breathe.

HOME IS SUBJECTIVE

You say home. I say cage.

CHAINED

Sometimes, I feel like a bird trying to fly with chained wings. My flight is locked.
I'm bound here, in more ways than one.

THE GRAVEYARD

The past was a haunted cemetery.
The ghosts liked to lounge around on the headstones,
colorless elbows propped on tops of legs that would swing
(back and forth and back and forth),
happily humming tunes that were familiar from my youth.
Lyrics that dripped Death,
notes that weren't afraid to knock on its door.
They'd sing and smile at me as I walked past,
a wicked knowing hardly hidden beneath the grins because
they knew I'd come back.
I always came back.
I knew every name in this graveyard.
Had walked the rows countless times and could do it blindfolded.
Would you like me to tell you of the first death? Her name was Peace.
It was her death that I took the hardest. The second, Joy;
she went soon after, as expected, because what other death could've
followed?
Of course, others went after them,
immeasurable deaths deemed minor until their remains became dust.
One of their names
(I'd never forget it)
was Laughter
(someone should've told him how special he was).

I remember all their deaths with vivid clarity,
the way one will always remember the nightmare that stays with them
no matter how many dreams follow after.
(That's what pain does; it brands.)
When they searched for a last breath they couldn't find,
I cradled their heads in my lap.
I watched their final tears roll from their stilling eyelids
(sad streams with lost direction).
I closed their stilled eyelids with trembling hands.
(Failed. I had failed to find the tears their compass.)
So many dead things.
I wasn't the murderer.
Still, they all belonged to me. Therefore,
the blood was on this child's hands.
(It had to be.)
And the ghosts treated me as such.

It's been a while since I've been to the graveyard.
I wonder if the ghosts still sing.

THE SWITCH

Wasn't gradual. Drop a glass and when it hits, it shatters into hundreds of pieces of itself, does it not?

VANITY

(Hm. Funny.)
The vanity mirror is cracked.
And it could almost remind me of the lightning in my gaze.
Yes, I've noticed it too.
A lawless anger...
Unchecked wrath maneuvers its way smoothly
along the edge of every word I speak.
Have you ever known syllables to have to walk a tightrope?
My tongue is coated in chilling words
birthed from the wound of silent frustration.
If only you knew.
There's a reason behind the storm
that lingers beneath my cold surface.
(But I'll have numbed you before you could figure it out.)
Living like a loose cannon
calls life to these dry bones.

TRUE LOVE

I know it with conditions.
I find it to be a close companion
when the strings reattach themselves to it on my behalf.
But Love, in its true form, is a stranger.
In the way I have come to know it,
this supposedly beautiful thing has unwritten rules
that I have broken myself to follow,
and will break myself for time and time again.
Because if I'm not broken, I'm something else
that is also strange.
I'm whole.
I want for nothing.
To put it simply, that scares me.
I have no reference; I don't remember a time
when I wasn't less than.
(Damaged, I should say. Never quite right. Too much or not
enough.)
You have the right to call me a coward.
(I've said it enough to the sad reflection that meets my mirror every
morning.)
But the fact of the matter is I am fragmented,
and pieces of me have traveled farther than I ever have.
I've accepted that I will never get them back.
(Another belief that's often spoken to the glass.)

Words like these take a long time to become unsaid,
especially when they're spoken to you, from you.
And I'm too far gone.
To believe that I will one day be loved
the way I have loved
is a joke in which the punchline no longer gets the laugh it used to.
I'd sooner believe the idea that the sky and the ground
would trade places.

A WEARY HAND WANTS TO REST HERE

Hope was an errant flame that took pleasure in burning her whenever she reached out.

SHADOWS

All I remember is music and what it told me,
back when days were dark and my mind was a scream. I was an aimless wanderer.
What was day, what was night.
Yesterday, today, tomorrow.
On any day, at any hour, I was perpetually alone.
Eventually, you get tired of swinging at the shadows.
So I lay down.
Rest assured, I didn't let them consume me.
I let them cover me. Just for a while.
As I lay there, underneath the covering of the ravens' wings, every once in a while
a melody would sneak through.
I could tell it had been looking for me and had traveled a long way to find me.
And though the notes were always different, the message remained the same:
"*It won't last.*"
I held onto what the notes told me.
(One year became two, two became three...)
I lay there until the words rang true.

UNTITLED

To feel your heart harden is strange.
The best way I can express what it felt like
is in one word: sharpening.
I was gaining edges.
My broken foundation began rebuilding itself with its own,
always unsteady hands.
(It still bothers me how suddenly it happened.)
Soon, I was completely made new, and one part of me
no longer had any distinction from the other.
All of me now shared one purpose: cut.
What else was dropped glass made to do?
My words drew blood.
My eyes never carried a threat that was empty.
The nature of my being was no longer one of warmth.
It was of warning.
To turn, before my eyes found you and the words made you their
next victim.
I hated it, but I took refuge in it. The blood on a blade was never its
own.
Most eventually took the warning well enough.
But of course, there's always one.
It had been a long time since there *had* been one and, at the thought,
somewhere inside of me,
I could feel a trace of the ancient warmth—
the opposite of my newfound haven, wanting to make itself known
again.

Laughter was his name.
We were strangers now but, once upon a time, he was a friend
(I'd known him better than most).
I'd almost forgotten how persistent he could be.
He visited me every day in various ways.
Especially at the times when I'd least expect. (Those were his favorite.)
Since his return, from that first day,
he was woven into all my days.
I was never caught off guard by his attempts but,
despite my best efforts,
that spark of warmth (of past things)
never went away.
From the first day, he'd waged a war
with who I now was.
I was unsure about whether or not I wanted him to succeed.
Though I had to admit, just to myself (never him),
that he was even more beautiful than the last time I'd seen him.
A very frightening realization, because one thing
was very obvious.
He was made to *oppose* me. To serve as a reminder.
(I never thought a day would come when we weren't on the same side.)
I stood still when he danced.
I pulled my hand away when he held his out.
Always.
As if he couldn't help it.
(I remembered the feeling.)

I frowned when he smiled, which is an act
that should be simple but when it came to him,
nothing ever was.
In his, you saw what you could be.
Its light was not an easy rising, like the dawn.
It wasn't the sun,
streaming through the trees and greeting the leaves on its way down
in the way only the sun can do so well.
It was anything but a clear and cloudless sky.
It was storms.
Storms that tempted with words of hope,
written and addressed to whatever remained of this heart,
that it could be what it once was.
(It could beat like it used to.)
The smile broke me in the way it feels to see an old friend
after 'all those' years. A familiar from which you can't shy away.
This was his way.
This was how Laughter got in.
Somewhere, near the warmth that wasn't dying
(as I once wished it to),
I felt a faint feeling of relief.
Very faint, but it was there.
I haven't forgotten the details.

The next thing I knew, the war was over.

Now

~ Now playlist ~

Rawnald Gregory Erickson the Second ~ STRFKR
To Love a Boy ~ Maya Hawke
What If ~ Beat The System
Hold Me Closer ~ RoneyBoys
Dirty Hippie ~ Alicia Blue
Eyes Without a Face ~ Billy Idol
Wilder Days ~ Morgan Wade
Heat Waves (with iann dior) ~ Glass Animals
cosmic (wait for me) ~ paris jackson
Never Again ~ Brett Gray
What Goes Around Comes Around ~ Michael Jackson
Secret ~ Joshua Bassett
Helium ~ Glass Animals
Life Goes On ~ BTS
Good Groovy Morning ~ Stereo Choir

THE RAINDROP ON THE WINDOW

In many ways, she felt like the raindrop on a car window. You know, *that* one. The lone one in the midst of all the others that finds the need to start its own pilgrimage.

It's a slow journey at first, a steady rhythm as it paces its footsteps to feel out the attitudes of those surrounding it. It doesn't want to appear unusual or uncanny. It hates the feeling of being out of place.

But after the drop has covered a little ground, the steps to this new rhythm no longer feel foreign. It might even discover a new confidence within itself... one that's not been fully built up. It's a tiny sliver in the making and a foretaste of what will soon make it whole, but the evidence of something it didn't know it had. All it needed to do was keep gently moving forward.

It continues. The rhythm is no longer gentle and steady, but gaining momentum. Apprehension is no longer a burden it drags along with it on its path. It grows with every stride it takes to a destination it doesn't know. It grows in dimension and confidence. It bounds past the lifeless, no longer fully afraid of the size it was meant to be, and keeps growing, expanding, and changing (dreaming). The drop maneuvers through the curves and grooves of its predestined path with a calm and unworried grace, both of which came easily when it quit being its own adversary.

The others have yet to learn: When your enemy is you, they stop fighting when you do.

The others sit. And wait. And wonder. And say "what if," never realizing that the only thing they have to do is begin moving.

The drop starts to move faster and faster, surprising itself with the speed at which it's learned to go. But an unwelcome question from the fearful mindset of its past arises.

Where am I going?

It feels forgotten habits and behaviors wanting to again take residence in their one-time home. These things felt far away to the drop now, but they still carried a hint of the eerie familiarity that always comes with unhealthy ways that have been deadened—familiarity that never feels good, but it's familiar nonetheless.

It smirks. Against the wishes of the prickly, edgy sensation—the bundle of fear with which it at one time felt as thick as thieves—it pushes forward. Its destination still unknown.

It knocks on the door of its fate. The door is heavily laden with endless possibilities. The opportunities it possesses radiate off it in waves. The drop need only walk through it once it opens and not let the door to its dreams close, especially after the distance it has traveled to see them again.

Past the door, fear has no place. The drop inhales. Exhales. And does what it was intended to do all along.

It begins to fashion itself into the grooves at the bottom of the window with no heaviness. It's never felt lighter. It makes itself amicable with this newfound terrain.

And it was never again seen by those who wished it had stayed still.

MOROSE

I've grown tired of the morose conversations.
Sadness and Unease had me as their playground in my younger days.
Fear, which walked aimlessly and constantly throughout the course of my being, gave the claws of a foreign horror an unyielding grip on my adolescent consciousness. That hold stole the last remains of my childlike naivety.
I've had enough of dark clouds.
Breathe life into me now.

ZIPPED LIPS

If they won't hear me, then I won't speak.
When I do, they'll be sorry they wished for my words.
But Time went on. With it, so did Life.
(Who told her it had better things to do than wait for her to stop wasting its presence.)
As they both went, she acquired the simple knowledge that a graceful word had the ability to venture further than a word replete with the animosity of an unhealed heart.
Its aim rang truer to the intended destination.
She could no longer fool herself into thinking the world around her deserved to be tinted dark with the colors that stained the sad moments of her story, the colors of unmended wounds that still swirled inside of her.

AN APOLOGY TO WHOM IT MAY CONCERN

For some of you,
my hips are too wide.
My legs are too small.
My skin is too light or too dark.
My feet are too flat.
My eyes are too brown.
My nose looks funny.
My hair is too nappy.
The gap between my teeth is too pronounced.
The childhood scars my legs have accumulated over time are excessive.
The way I speak is too slow.
The way I speak is too quiet.
And the way I dress is weird.

That being said,
I am sorry I do not fit into your imperfect vision of what perfect is supposed to look like.
I am not sorry, however, that I no longer feel bad about it.

A LETTER TO THE DOLL

If I could go back to the dying doll,
I'd give her the hug she needed to hold her together.
Maybe it would have been unwise to hug shattered glass, but I
would've risked the cuts
for that doll and told her she was more than shards.
She wasn't made to wound. She was made for the opposite,
and eventually she'd get back there.
But until she did, I would've glued her,
and she probably wouldn't have liked that much either
because her scars would still be evident and obvious
and you'd still see that she'd been dropped.
But deep down, she would've thanked me
because I'd helped her until she was back
 to who she was supposed to be.

One day, the doll made up her mind that she wasn't ready to die yet.
So here I am.
If I could go back to the doll, on that day,
I'd give her the hug I needed to tell her thank you.

TWENTY-TWO

The first year I've known what complete happiness and complete joy felt like.
Pretty pitiful track record for the person named Joyah.
It's not all life's fault: I allowed the past parts of it to manipulate the good spirit of whatever was going on in the present. I'd let myself be happy *to an extent* and enjoy *some*.
I lived never completely attached to the joy of my surroundings, just in case the rug was pulled from underneath and I had to let it go.
I've been both of these things: *half-happy/hungry for joy* and *completely unhappy/starved of joy*.
I don't know which is worse, but I knew if I kept living the reality of either one, I would never find peace.
It took a while to get to that point, but I'm glad I was finally able to reach it.
I'm no longer scared to walk through life in fear that, one day, my feet won't find solid ground.
I guess this is a letter of sorts to those who are scared like I was.
I hope and pray you find the courage to allow yourself the peace of confidently walking forward.

MUSIC

Initially, I'd call ours a curious love affair. But no one's ever loved me like you have.
You met me in the mire of my brokenness.
You didn't dismiss the fragments I'd been left in, but you chose to see the pieces before they were pieces.
Amid my fragments, you still saw a song;
beneath the mud of my forsaken devastations, you saw a glimpse of the timid melodies and soft chords life wrought out of me with its heavy blows. You saw the 'more' in me my eyes couldn't see.
You took the timidity from the notes in my bones and made me unafraid.
You did not steal my softness, but watered it, and meekness grew;
you gave me a quiet strength. I didn't know you'd become a most trusted companion.
You've taken the sweet time to learn every part of me and in doing that, you've shown me a beautiful patience that continues to take my breath away.
Admittedly, I never pictured you in my life in this way. Now, I can't imagine one of my days without the hint of your smile.
The brightness of your smile acts as my sun.
I'm awaiting the day the words are invented that will allow me to properly expound on how it casts its subtle yet encompassing warmth upon my skin and brings radiance to my days.

You're the paved destiny I wasn't always sure of. The pen with which I tell my stories.
I love you always.

MUSIC II

Your love for me is boundless and with you, I move past horizons.

WINGS

I look up and wonder:
Should I ask the angel if he'd trade places?
He answers my unspoken question in the nudge of my best friend's shoulder
against mine as we sit and watch the sun set.
Wearing soft smiles as the light reflects across our faces in hues of orange.

Another day.
I think about asking him while I'm walking when, all of a sudden,
I hear a song I haven't heard in a long time.
My heart lovingly recognizes it as one of the songs that
used to carry me.

Another day.
I think about asking him because the question is beginning to burn my lungs,
"What's it like to have feet that walk roads paved with gold
instead of feet forced to walk among souls desiring to add weight to yours?"
I want to ask him what it's like to carry wings on his back in the place of heavy burdens.
He never has to cry and has never been laid down by life.
How does it feel?

I never ask him.

He knows that my question is always answered in the little things, so he'll bring something like the flowers to my attention, and I'll notice that they carry a bit more beauty with them than they did the day before.

I'll see that all of the trees have scattered colors: reds, greens, oranges. A bit of gold.

The wind speaks to them and they listen, and it's a beautiful thing.

The sky looks down on me and its lips slowly split into a grin, eager to reveal its new shade of blue.

THE SONGBIRD

I don't think my love for you can be measured,
but I guess the closest estimate
would be the miles I would have to cover
to wrap around the entirety of this world
and all of the beauty in it that goes unseen.
The shape of you has disappeared from view
and your wings have faded into the sunset,
but your radiance still stains my life
in colors that can only bleed from a soul set apart.
And be brushed onto the canvas of a soul just the same.
Thank you for everything.

PURPLE ACOUSTIC

If I knew you were hidden beneath the melody,
I would've sung this song a long time ago.
In the beginning, my heart made out the sound of a sweet soul's crooning,
and a ballad of love stories yet untold ebbed and flowed from my fingertips,
as they mindlessly strummed the song that is you without even knowing it.
I hold a special admiration for the way you effortlessly wove your way into my strings
and stowed away inside them until you were ready to make your notes known to me.
My heart knew you before I did.
Which is why I guess, eventually, it couldn't help but sing
in accompaniment with the newly-discovered song that streamed from my fingers
with the uncomplicated ease of one who's played this song before.
You were the first song I ever knew in more ways than one.
The only song my purple acoustic ever bothered to play.

<33

~ <33 playlist ~

Live It Up ~ Jermaine Jackson
The Love You Save ~ The Jackson 5
There She Goes ~ The La's
Do You Believe in Magic ~ The Lovin' Spoonful
For Once I Can Say ~ Sophia James
She Loves You ~ The Beatles
Beginning Middle End (from the Netflix Film "To All The Boys: Always and Forever") ~ The Greeting Committee
My Jinji ~ Sunset Rollercoaster
I Wanna Be Where You Are (Live in Japan/1973) ~ The Jackson 5

NEVER BEEN KISSED

Your lips are nice; I wish I knew what to do with them.

BLINK

Blink and you'll miss it.
But if you have a moment, watch her
just for a second because a second's worth of her true affection
is all she'll allow to the surface, anyway.
Watch the way her eyes change when he walks into a room.
The light that appears. Everyone sees it except him,
which is ironic, in the sad way.
How are you blind to light that only you bring,
bright enough to make the stars doubt themselves?
But the stars never get the chance, nor the chance to turn
the palest shade of green with envy.
They watch her hide the light as quickly as it shines to the surface.

CRUSH

One day, his name was simply written across her heart,
though nothing was simple about the feeling.
I should rephrase.
It was less of a feeling and more of a knowing, an instinct.
One look, and he'd become as natural to her as breathing.
His eyes held the warmth with which she'd long dreamed of being embraced.
His smile held Time in its hand;
its effortless beauty made days pass
as though they weren't days at all,
but merely moments when the sun decided it needed
to rest from the sky and sit with her for a while.
Looking at it for too long, she'd always lose her concept of Time,
which was a welcome change from the slow pace of Heartache
to which she'd grown accustomed.
Not only that, it was bright enough to bring the light back into her eyes.
She pondered at how ordinary features we've become so used to
could have such an extraordinarily profound effect on her.
As if every time she sees them,
she's seeing them for the first time.
"How on Earth am I going to get out of this one?" she'd question herself,
day in and day out.

She fought it at first.
Tried to erase the name that seemed to be written with enduring ink across every beat of her heart since that fateful day.
But she knew it was a losing battle.
So instead, she let her fists rest.
And welcomed the handwriting of the pen.
Shame he was clueless.

IF ONLY YOU KNEW

Before it knew you,
It had no fireplace to warm at on the cold nights,
no shelves lined with worn and well-loved books with broken spines,
no windows to look out and admire the morning dew that rested softly on the grass in the early hours.

Before it knew you, it was timeworn walls and weak floors.
All of its pictures laid astray and sought escape from the battered frames.
The rooms were hollow in spirit and mourned for what they once carried in their corners.
The house still stood, but only as an act of defiance against those who wished to see it torn down.

The very thought of you staggers me.
My heart is a home because of you.

_____ AT ITS FINEST

What she said, what she left unsaid.
That was the slow death.
A mouth that speaks words, but pretty words. Filtered words.
Correct words that held no risk.
She hated those words. They didn't belong to her, tasted funny, and made her feel worse than they tasted.
No one understood. The love inside her had no refinement... no sophistication.
It was unbridled. Passionate disorder, welcomed by her with open arms.
From her long road of sorrows,
she'd been molded
for a capacity to love beyond the unspoken boundaries.
No one understood.
Choice had no part in this: What was free will to fixed chaos?
And how deep it ran, and kept running.
Think past the shallow waters, beyond the surface of skin.
The expanse of it, the weight of it
are why it only calls on a soul that's been severed a certain kind of way.

Few have been chosen to experience this fate that, on occasion, seems the most twisted.
Some people call them 'the lucky ones.'
They still don't know whether to call themselves cursed or blessed.

Loose me, it cries, and the cry burns her every inhale and exhale. This madness that begged made *her* mad.

How are you today? What she said.

You are not my missing piece. "Missing" implies something was lost to be found, but I never lost you. How could I lose something that was always of me, even in the days I was naively unaware?
You don't "complete" me because you can't complete what you've been part of since the very beginning.
You are as much of me as I am of you, and without one, the other—.
The madness leaves when you're here; you're its peace and quiet. What she left unsaid.

MISSED OPPORTUNITIES

Say it.
She'd had enough of this.
Soft brushes of fingertips, an accidental graze of the knee.
Words that never spoke beyond the limits of the unspoken rules of this unspoken game they had both determined within themselves to play.
The stares that always said more than words did.
The air, palpable with the tension of words unsaid.
She had become drained by this.
If three words, eight letters, out in the open with no place to hide was what it meant to lose, she would lose everything.
Over and over, for him, she'd never win and do it gladly.

THE ANSWER TO YOUR QUESTION

"What do you want?"

That's a weighted question.
Each answer is heavier than the last
because every one of them is attached
to the first.
You.

FOR YOU

I hate it.
I can't write you.
It doesn't matter how many of these things I finish.
Every time I look back at them, I get angry.
I can't see you in any of them, yet I can see you clearly.
You're in all the words, and you're in none of them.
I have never felt this frustrated.
With all the love poems, stories, and sonnets in the world,
here I am,
sitting with a pen and a measly sheet of paper,
trying to get the black ink to say words that haven't been invented yet.
You are seamlessly woven into my oxygen,
and I hate the words even as I write them down
because it's still not enough.
I can't write the way your smile shifts dimensions.
I so easily define you and then I wake up.
The slate is clean, and you've changed again.
I'm meeting a stranger, yet I'm greeting my best friend.

UNIQUE

You are one of the unique souls mine was tailor-made to love.

Others

~ Others playlist ~

All Time Low ~ Jon Bellion
Please Don't Go ~ Joel Adams
Not Thinkin' Bout You ~ Ruel
Ghost Of You ~ 5 Seconds of Summer
Follow the River ~ Calexico
Home ~ Catie Turner
Low C ~ Supergrass
breathe again ~ paris jackson

AUTUMN OUTFIT

The top toggle button on her trench coat caught the glint of light coming from the couple's eyes across the way.

She averted her eyes and pretended she didn't see it, too.

The knitted sweater she was wearing beneath it reminded her of their first Christmas together, probably because he had bought her those gloves to match.

The blue jeans she was wearing still held the dampness from the few tears that had escaped her eyes in the coffee shop, an embarrassing act she would probably never let herself live down.

The boots she was wearing, her favorite worn, brown leathers, were beginning to show their age. Time was wearing them down, just like her, but not enough to miss the footfalls of Love that had walked these streets before. This place was teeming with Love. Such a shame it's no longer familiar to the wearer. If it were at this moment to turn the corner, walk down the street, and introduce itself, she wouldn't recognize it.

She would *pretend* not to.

Her falling out with Love wasn't a gradual transition. How do relationship transitions in life normally go? Maybe: best friend, to good friend, to friend, to acquaintance, to happy stranger.

But her falling out with Love had been a clean cut. Supposedly. She'd convinced herself the cut hadn't left a scar, but *deep* down she knew her heart still had jagged edges where the cut was not quite as clean as she'd fooled herself it was.

The necklace she was wearing brought forth memories. Whether they were memories she longed to forget or memories she longed to never forget, she didn't honestly know, but she'd done her best to figure it out since his absence.
The ring she was no longer wearing was what had finally brought all the tears past the surface of her façade. He'd proposed around this time last year.

She took her ring finger in her hand and felt the ghost of where Love used to be.

VISIT

Dead petals scatter along the ground in the gentle winds.
Wind was the only thing able to carry me here.
I wish I could come around to visit you more often.
I just hope you understand that it's difficult to make it past the
blurry vision and the slight shake my hands always seem to get when
I read your name carved into stone.
My mind always travels to the thought that you're a cold, empty
husk six feet underneath the ground. A shell of who you were in the
most literal sense.
I remember the countless days I used to wish for you to be this way.
I guess I should've remembered that the wishes with the greatest
chance of being granted are the twisted ones.

IT MOVES AGAINST MY WILL

Strange feeling to always write words
that never belong to me.

RIBS

I overheard your conversation on the phone that day.
You said he'd bruised your ribs.
Given you another black eye.
No matter how hard I tried not to, I met your eyes;
it was the sad kind of vulnerability
to fracture a heart on the spot, make it turn its lips down.
Eyes that looked like they wanted to cry,
but didn't want to waste the time.
I find it interesting to realize now that you weren't actually
whispering.
It wasn't a real whisper; it was a whisper meant for the stage,
almost like you wanted to be heard.
I hope you were.
Not just by the ears of a stranger's child with nothing
to offer but her childlike compassion and eyes of curiosity,
but by the ears of someone who wouldn't shy away.

SANDS

I want you to give me something to hold on to.
I'm scared of a love that can slip
through my fingers and mimic the sands.
Fragile.
Taking the shape of whatever environment is holding it.
A love on borrowed time.

SHE ROTS

Vines twine where the children used to be.
Nothing has grown in the garden for a long, long time.
Try as you might,
you still cannot hate the old crone.
Tilt your head and listen.
Closely.
Do you hear them, like I do every day?
Her bones are weeping.
Almost as loudly as the bones of these walls
she calls a house because she can no longer call them a home.
Almost as loudly as the bones of her past,
when light was still a thing that her life could hold on to.
(The light has run.)
The shackles she has chosen for herself...
their groans keep me awake at night.
They weep just as the bones do.
Tell me how.
How can they, the bones, cry?
How can walls allow tears to stain them
as if they were like us?
(Like us. To cry for what they once were.
Lament for what they will never be.
A heart broken in halves, Past and Present.
Like us.)
They do it because she does not.
They are dying because she can't.

There are two ways to live forever:
in the love you've sown or in the hatred.
It makes me sad that this is the way
she'll withstand the test of time.
Hatred has made her immortal.
Mortality was beaten with the price of her heart.
The living dead.

Acknowledgements

Thank you God, for giving me this book and for doing it when You did.

Thank you Reyna Pellegrin, for the beautiful cover art (and for the espresso).

Thank you M.A. Rehman, for bringing the entire cover together.

Thank you Kathryn Palmer, for being an editing dream.

Thank you family + friends. Your excitement for this lil' ole project of mine was never overlooked or unappreciated.

Thank you, person who picked this up. You're pretty cool.

About the Author

Joyah Claiborne is an NYT bestselling author of a number of titles, some of which include:

Totally kidding; this is my first book. Written somewhere between dozens of chocolate chip cookies, avoiding the insufferable Southern sun, and playing with my dog Yazmine (sweetest dog in the world AND her social battery is smaller than mine. She's an introvert's dream).

But if this one somehow managed to persuade you to stick around, in addition to my undoubtedly sparkling personality, follow me if you'd like on IG: @joyyy_reads.

Copyright ©2024 Joyah Aleyxsis Claiborne, Aleyxsis Publishing
All rights reserved. No part of this book may be reproduced, stored, or transmitted in any form by any means—electronic, mechanical, photocopy, recording, or otherwise—without the express written permission of the publisher.

www.ingramcontent.com/pod-product-compliance
Lightning Source LLC
Chambersburg PA
CBHW030453100526
44580CB00006B/105/J